Sanctum of Shadows

Volume III

Spiritus Occultus

Aleister Nacht

SANCTUM OF SHADOWS · SPIRITUS OCCULTUS

© 2017 ALEISTER NACHT

PUBLISHED BY
LOKI / SPECKBOHNE PUBLISHING

NO PART OF THIS BOOK MAY BE REPRODUCED BY ANY MEANS WITHOUT PRIOR WRITTEN PERMISSION OF THE BOOK PUBLISHER.

ALL RIGHTS RESERVED

ISBN-10: 0-9903693-1-5
ISBN-13: 978-0-9903693-1-8

FIRST EDITION PRINT
10 9 8 7 6 5 4 3 2 1
UNITED STATES OF AMERICA

Connect with Aleister Nacht

Website
AleisterNacht.com

Satanic Magic Blog
SatanicMagic.Wordpress.com

Facebook
facebook.com/Aleister.Nacht.Books

Twitter
Twitter.com/AleisterNacht

Dark Arts Forum
Proboards.com/login/3550189

YouTube
YouTube.com/user/SatanicAudioBlog

THIS BOOK IS DEDICATED TO THE MEMBERS OF THE
MAGNUM OPUS SATANIC COVEN.
SCIO, IPSE VENIT.

"THE DANGER OF BECOMING MISOLOGISTS OR HATERS OF ARGUMENT," SAID HE, "AS PEOPLE BECOME MISANTHROPISTS OR HATERS OF MAN; FOR NO WORSE EVIL CAN HAPPEN TO A MAN THAN TO HATE ARGUMENT. MISOLOGY AND MISANTHROPY ARISE FROM SIMILAR CAUSES. FOR MISANTHROPY ARISES FROM TRUSTING SOMEONE IMPLICITLY WITHOUT SUFFICIENT KNOWLEDGE."[1]

PLATO

[1] *Plato in Twelve Volumes, Vol. 1 translated by Harold North Fowler; Introduction by W.R.M. Lamb. Cambridge, MA, Harvard University Press; London, William Heinemann Ltd. 1966.*

SANCTUM OF SHADOWS · SPIRITUS OCCULTUS

Nomina Actorum

EXULTATION	9
PRAELUDIUM	11
PARS I - ARGUMENTUM	13
CUM GRANO SALIS	23
FALSUS VETUSTAS	29
SOLVE ET COAGULA	39
PARS II - SPIRITUS INFERNUM	57
SATHANAS NOS LIBERAVIT	73
IMMORTUI	79
AVE VERSUS CHRISTI	83
EPILOGUS	87
SCIRE QUOD SCIENDUM	89
ECCE HOMO	103

"In our world today, we wield an ink pen in much the same way that, in years past, the sword was used. We use it to cut people into small pieces; we use it to end their career; end their life; end their freedom and, as a person, make them disappear forever."[2]

---

[2] *Sanctum of Shadows Volume I The Satanist*

EXULTATION

Black Angels sing from kingdom depths
Adorned in cloaks of cashmere and satin
Chalice of elixir and athame of bone

Candles of black and altar of flesh
Time nevermore, eve of his accession
No longer exiled, now beguiled by all

Hypnotic spells of bewitchment
Lords and Dukes smile, vestal virgins bow
Our congregation obeisance pays

We usher in His celestial Satanic Age
Once anathema, darkness becomes flesh
All shall worship Him and whisper
His name in majestic reverence

An Heir to Dynasty at last rules
To an abyss with fraudulent humanity
These cattle nearing an abattoir

Hail Satan!

"WERDE, DER DU BIST."
FRIEDRICH NIETZSCHE

"SUPERSTITION IS THE RELIGION OF FEEBLE MINDS."
EDMUND BURKE

Praeludium

I. Satan, we ask for your divine guidance to open the gates of infernal wisdom.

II. Satan, rise from Hell to your rightful throne above the heavens of those who cast truth asunder.

III. Leviathan, Belial, Azazel! Let your knowledge shine brightly to light our way in this world subdued by ignorance.

IV. Lucifer, we build your altar of illumination amongst the thorns and thistles of lascivious hate.

V. Shaitan, we have come to sow our seeds into barren chambers and usher your Satanic arrival triumphus.

VI. Zepar, Balan, Räum, Caym, Perchta! Demons of old, come forth and reveal your wisdom and fulfill your desires; consecro!

VII. Sathanas, we shall boldly rip their temple veil bottom to top and procure your celestial tribunal.

VIII. Beelzebub, we shall impeach futile resistance and forever silence their ancient aspersions of our true majesty.

IX. Satan, devour their dominion and break the vassal chains of our silence to allow truth to finally be known to all.

X. Nephilim of old, disgrace and dishonor those once called "unblemished" and "chosen", finally revealing their hoax, defamation, and true motivations.

XI. Astaroth, cast down their star so it will be shattered, splintered, and scattered forever upon the ephemeral winds.

XII. Alastor, the dust of pulverized bones shall pave the established pathway; far to the left and travelled in search of Satanic enlightenment.

XIII. Satan, never again shall their lies be considered factual; their propaganda, lecherous attacks, and fallacious bloodlines revealed.

SANCTUM OF SHADOWS · SPIRITUS OCCULTUS

PARS I - ARGUMENTUM

WHAT IF THEY ARE MISTAKEN?
WHAT IF THE ACCEPTED AUTHORITIES ARE WRONG?

What would change in your belief system if you found out the established and recognized experts were proven to be frauds; their statements of fact questionable; their logical assertions flawed and incorrect? Could it be that we have been deceived by arrogance?

Society looks to the subject matter experts in their chosen field to be the "all knowing" individuals. We buy their theories, hypotheses, and opinions. We plan our daily lives according to their information about the past, present, and future.

All that hold dear, relevant, important, and evident are formed on the basis of savvy experts, advisors, authorities, connoisseurs, professionals, gurus, buffs, etc., who provide suggestions, guidance, recommendations, etc. What if these obdurate counselors were providing disinformation or misinformation; either intentionally or unintentionally?

Throughout history, humans have thought they were right and even swore to that without having factual foundations and ultimately

BEING PROVEN WRONG.

EVERYONE IS SELLING SOMETHING; EXPERTS AND AUTHORITIES ARE NO DIFFERENT, SELLING IDEAS AND ADVICE. SOME PROVIDE PLAUSIBLE INFORMATION, SOME PROVIDE JUSTIFICATIONS, AND SOME PROVIDE DATA TO SUPPORT THEIR POSITIONS.

IF THE INFORMATION AND SUPPORTING EVIDENCE SEEMS TO ALIGN, MOST PEOPLE WILL ACCEPT SUCH IDEAS AS FACTS EVEN WHEN THERE SEEMS TO BE GLARING CONTRADICTIONS AND / OR INCONSISTENCIES.

WHY DOES THIS HAPPEN? BETTER YET, HOW CAN A PERSON PREVENT BEING FOOLED INTO BELIEVING A LIE? IS IT A NEED TO CONFORM, DESIRE TO BELIEVE IN FELLOW-HUMANITY, HERD MENTALITY, OR SOMETHING MORE OMINOUS? IS THERE REALLY A 'DUBIOUS AUTHORITY'? SOMETIMES FICTION IS MORE DIGESTIBLE AND PALATABLE THAN TRUTH.

HUMANITY HAS NOT ENJOYED A 'STELLAR RECORD' WHEN TRUTH IS THE ISSUE AT HAND. WE SOMEHOW FEEL OBLIGATED TO BELIEVE WHAT IS HEARD REGARDLESS OF WHAT IS KNOWN, SEEN, OR BELIEVED. THIS HAS LEAD TO SOME OF THE MOST BRUTAL AND TRAGIC ERAS IN OUR COLLECTIVE HISTORY.

STILL, OUR HISTORY CONTINUES TO 'REPEAT ITSELF' IN A NEVER-ENDING CYCLE OF LIES, DECEPTION, AND INFLUENCES ATTRIBUTED TO AUTHORITY FIGURES AND EXPERTS. ARE HUMANS NOT SUPPOSED TO LEARN FROM MISTAKES OR ARE WE DOOMED TO PLAY OUT THE SAME script with the same characters and only a change of actors? Are we becoming enlightened or simply 'blinded by the light'?

Many arguments have been presented as undeniable truth by established religions. These assertions begin as deductive or inductive, attempting to justify the position based upon a premise and objective evidence. Lacking true and valid conclusions, these assertions quickly become logically fallacious with conclusions devolving into mere assumption supported by dubious authority, distraction, or ad hominem arguments.

Some religious zealots expect total submission, disregarding any logical justification by begging the question and application of force.

From the protection of conjecture, a religiously flawed syllogism permits the orator to argue in foro conscientiae and appeal to like-minded idealists, creating a perilous theological slippery slope, absent of critical thought or deductive reason.

Whether modus ponens or modus tollens, affirmation or denial may be fabricated resulting in a 'reductio ad absurdum' misology as illustrated in Socrates' demise.

Neither axioms nor tautologies exist which

are absolute, unequivocal, or unquestionable concerning religious arguments. Inevitably, one or more of the premises will certainly be flawed due to subjectivity and personal bias.

It is difficult for the human animal to separate fact from emotional belief and this fallacy often results in the maintenance of an unsound (invalid) argument, regardless of plausibility or inductive logic of any hypothesis at question.

Inconsistencies or contradictions often result in an embarrassing paradox disproving the asserted premises or inferences based upon ambiguity, evasion, distraction, or lack of evidentiary logic.

Redirection or 'shifting' conclusions are easily overlooked when presented as a valid argument. This may result in a frustratingly flawed and paradoxical conclusion when terms supporting the premises are ambiguous or suddenly change meaning. Consider the following syllogism.

> People with imaginations are free.
> Prisoners are free to use imagination.
> Therefore, prisoners are free.

Christians have based conversionary arguments upon sacred truths cited from their biblical scriptures. However, this argument requires acceptance of the Bible as a document of authority. The conclusion of this argument is defective because the scriptures supporting their sacred truths are based upon an accepted, yet unproven, premise. So begins a poisonous intubation.

Often the person presenting the argument will attempt to justify the willful omission of pertinent information as a 'means to an end' (Zweckrationalität[3]) to save the souls of mankind however, this reasoning is a de facto lie. Although convictions may be sincere, the conclusion and justification is defective due to misrepresentation of facts by omission.

An incoherent paradox employed in argument serves as distraction by attempting to connect unrelated claims to illustrate a point. This myopic technique drones away without conclusion (The Arrow Paradox[4]).

Anselm's Proslogion[5] ad hominem ontological argument serves as an example of redirection and personal attack by beginning his

---

[3] *A Defense of Religious Exclusivism; Alvin Plantinga*

[4] *Aristotle Physics, 239b.30*

[5] *Monologion and Proslogion, with replies of Gaunilo and Anselm; Thomas Williams*

ARGUMENT BY INSULTING THE ENTIRE READERSHIP. ALAS, THE "IN YOUR FACE" METHODOLOGY IS AS SUBTLE (AND UNINTELLIGENT) AS REALITY TELEVISION.

PERHAPS TO SPARE THE READER MORE OF MY TAUTOLOGOUS POINTS, I SHOULD PROCEED TO THE HYPOTHESES PRESENTED IN THIS BOOK. DURING MY RESEARCH, I FOUND CERTAIN CHRONOLOGICALLY COHERENT OCCURRENCES WHICH MAY BE PARADOXICAL OR SIMPLY COINCIDENCE. I WILL PRESENT MY HYPOTHESIS, PROVIDE COMMENTARY, AND MY CONCLUSION FOR SOME OF THESE ANOMALIES. IT IS FOR THE READER TO DECIDE HER / HIS OPINION: MAJORITY OPINION OR DISSENTING OPINION.

IN THIS BOOK, I EXPLORE THE QUESTION OF TRUTH AND PERCEPTION WHILE USING MY IDEAS TO ILLUSTRATE CONCLUSIONS. I BELIEVE A SATANIST MUST BE KNOWLEDGABLE AND ASTUTE; ALWAYS QUESTIONING

UNTIL SATISFIED.

THIS BOOK OPENS THE ARENA OF COGNITIVE COMBAT TO ALLOW THE SATANIST TO INTELLIGENTLY ENGAGE IN 'THOUGHT' AND ARGUMENT, TO FACILITATE BETTER UNDERSTANDING OF VALIDATION, WHILE ACCEPTING OR REJECTING A PREMISE BASED UPON EVIDENCE, REASONING, AND PERSONAL EXPERIENCE.

TO PREVENT THE EFFECT OF 'BOILING THE OCEAN', I HAVE SELECTED SOME LESSER-KNOWN HISTORICAL EVENTS TO ANALYZE. IF YOU ARE LOOKING FOR THE SECRETS OF SATANIC RITUAL OR MAGIC, THIS BOOK WILL LEAVE YOU ASKING "WHAT JUST HAPPENED?" BECAUSE YOU WILL NOT FIND THAT INFORMATION HEREIN. THE SCOPE OF SUBJECT MATTER MUST BE LIMITED TO ALLOW ADEQUATE CONSUMPTION AND DIGESTION.

YOU WILL HOWEVER, FIND AN EXPLORATION OF HUMANITY AND MAGIC, INCLUDING THE HISTORICAL LANDSCAPE COMPLETE WITH HUMAN REMAINS LITTERING THE TOPOGRAPHY. PLEASE WATCH YOUR STEP............

PERHAPS WE SHOULD BEGIN WITH A QUICK DEFINITION OF 'OCCULTUS', AS APPLIED IN THIS BOOK. OCCULTUS MEANS 'HIDDEN OR SECRETLY CONCEALED' WHICH IN THIS CONTEXT IS EXACTLY HOW IT IS APPLIED WITHIN THIS BOOK; THINK OF THE CONTENTS AS A GUIDED DISCUSSION WITH A LIBERAL APPLICATION OF THE SOCRATIC METHOD OF TEACHING THAT PULLS INSTEAD OF PUSHES THE STRING OF DISCOVERY.

Next, the word 'Argumentum' is a 'methodical appeal to reason using theory, supposition, premise, and evidence'. Some of you may recognize the construction of arguments from your freshman or sophomore year in college and the subject has certainly not become more exciting in the interim however, it seems to be time-tested as an accepted way to present ideas, invoke thought, and provoke discussions. Perhaps this book will do all three.

The world is holistically changing by cumulative effect. Perhaps past and present academics have made assumptions that are wrong or consisted of flawed premises and conclusions. The past civilizations may have actually known more about the world around them than we do today. Certainly this hypothesis 'flies in the face' or modern egotistical academics.

'Free will' is always a factor since nothing is preordained in our physical world. We cannot change lunar cycles or turn day into night however, we can attempt to understand, adapt our reality to the circumstances, and decide to embrace or reject based upon objective evidence and serious consideration. Instead of material wealth, what if knowledge and enlightenment were the lofty goals and the attainment of both was the objective of humanity as a whole? How would that world look to all of us?

You may notice two common themes in this book. One is a concept of 'hidden in plain site' and the second is 'belief formed through the application of reasoning'. I could have easily used arguments for the best tasting hot sauce, Apple versus Microsoft, or the greatest heavy metal band in the world. The examples may provide some insight or information you were unaware of however, the objective is to lead the Satanic neophyte to reach his / her own conclusion as a product of reasoning application.

The Spiritus (Spirit) is examined from a position of fulfillment; the gaping hole in the human self-center which presents questions forever begging for answers. The human mind is the most powerful of our evolutionary tools and yet, many simply refuse to explore its power or develop its vast and limitless possibilities.

Self preservation and defense mechanisms force many to dismiss the existence of celestial beings, thus protecting the psyche from the perceived weakness of vulnerability. Some feel better by simply refusing to believe anything beyond the physical three-dimensional boundaries.

Let's begin and extirpate falsity in search of "Valore Intrinseco", without the appeal of authority; allowing you to decide these matters for yourself.

Children of the grave, Satanic Blessings!

Aleister Nacht
31 October 2016

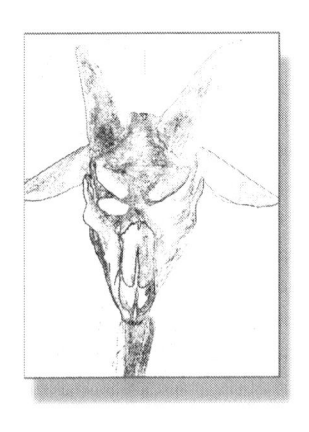

Cum Grano Salis

Power tends to corrupt (Lord Acton).
Knowledge is power (Francis Bacon).
Therefore knowledge tends to corrupt.[6]

The argument above is an example of Informal Fallacy which has been used to manipulate the subject matter and change the overall meaning. While it is certainly a valid argument in structure and form according to the rules of inference however, the conclusion is paradoxical.

The subtle ambiguity in meaning coupled with a redirection could certainly allow this conclusion to go unchecked, especially if 'authoritative distractors' were added to the argument. If confusing scientific terms and changing meanings were also employed, a person may easily be convinced that the conclusion is

---

[6] Irving M. Copi, *Informal Logic*, 7th ed.

DEDUCTIVELY PLAUSIBLE.

GRANTED, THIS ARGUMENT IS UNDERSTANDABLE TO THE POPULOUS HOWEVER, WHAT IF THE SUBJECT MATTER IS NOT SO EASILY UNDERSTOOD?

IN 'A SCIENTIFIC ARGUMENT FOR THE EXISTENCE OF GOD[7]', ROBIN COLLINS USES THE FOLLOWING IN SUPPORT OF THE FINE TUNING ARGUMENT.

"THE FORCE OF GRAVITY IS DETERMINED BY NEWTON'S LAW $F = GM_1M_2/R^2$. HERE G IS WHAT IS KNOWN AS THE GRAVITATIONAL CONSTANT, AND IS BASICALLY A NUMBER THAT DETERMINES THE FORCE OF GRAVITY IN ANY GIVEN CIRCUMSTANCE. FOR INSTANCE, THE GRAVITATIONAL ATTRACTION BETWEEN THE MOON AND THE EARTH IS GIVEN BY FIRST MULTIPLYING THE MASS OF THE MOON (M_1) TIMES THE MASS OF THE EARTH (M_2), AND THEN DIVIDING BY THE DISTANCE BETWEEN THEM SQUARED (R^2). FINALLY, ONE MULTIPLIES THIS RESULT BY THE NUMBER G TO OBTAIN THE TOTAL FORCE. CLEARLY THE FORCE IS DIRECTLY PROPORTIONAL TO G: FOR EXAMPLE, IF G WERE TO DOUBLE, THE FORCE BETWEEN THE MOON AND THE EARTH WOULD DOUBLE."[8]

IF YOU UNDERSTAND AND CAN APPLY THE ABOVE, YOU ARE IN THE MINORITY. SOME MAY WANT TO

---

[7] *A Scientific Argument for the Existence of God*

[8] *https://www.discovery.org/a/91*

engage in this argument however, the subject matter may be 'above their heads' on a cognitive level. Others may totally dismiss this argument as conjecture or may simply discount it as irrelevant.

Some may attempt to "bluff" their way through this argument; having neither the mental faculty nor academic training necessary to provide an intellectual viewpoint. To quickly evaluate the audience, perhaps the following could be substituted.

"For instance, the gravitational attraction between the moon and the earth is given by first multiplying the mass of the moon (M2) times the mass of the earth (M1), and then dividing by the distance between them (R)."

If challenged, the author could simply claim this was a typographical error; an honest mistake. You may call it 'the shell game' or 'bait and switch'; by whatever name, it will certainly separate the casual bystanders and novice science 'geeks' from the truly knowledgable.

Arguments should be neither hostile nor offensive. An argument should be clear and to others to ship to self and others. An argument should be based upon mutual respect on a personal level. Those are the most effective arguments.

If your opinion is important and deserves the best supporting argument. If you are trying to persuade someone with a sound premise and valid conclusion you should spend enough time to prepare your argument well. Using a brute fact will not gain the advantage intellectually.

There are those who think that Appeal to Force (argumentum ad baculum) will prove an argument and many times an argument devolves into not only a heated debate but a physical altercation.

These altercations are usually provoked by those who are losing the argument and as a byproduct, have allowed themselves to become emotionally invested. An argument should not result in beating someone into submission.

In some cases, valid arguments have been suppressed due to 'analysis paralysis'. This happens when the discoverer of the idea is simply afraid to bring forth the idea and introduce it in a public forum.

Nevertheless, consideration of all perspectives is certainly required to fully understand a concept and arrive at a valid conclusion.

SANCTUM OF SHADOWS · SPIRITUS OCCULTUS

PREMATURE DISMISSAL OF ANY AVAILABLE INFORMATION WILL CERTAINLY LEAD TO AN INACCURATE CONCLUSION FAUX PAS.

WITCH

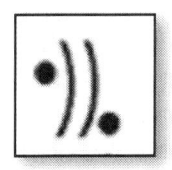

SANCTUM OF SHADOWS · SPIRITUS OCCULTUS

Falsus Vetustas

"History is written by the victors."
Winston Churchill

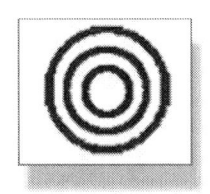

Argument: "Intelligent civilizations have existed long before the timelines provided by contemporary authorities."

Most contemporary experts consider the world civilization of mankind to be between 5000 and 6000 years old. This estimation of time fits well with the commonly accepted academic timeline of human evolution. Although it is a convenient chronology which fits into the historical hypothesis, does not mean it is true or beyond questioning.

Plato defined his "Great Year" as a cycle of 26,000 years, or one eon. Sir Isaac Newton even wrote a book about procession, which attempted to align history with the stars and celestial movements. His writings support a much longer period of history than 5000 or 6000 years.

Obviously, Newton's theory was discounted and wiped out because it simply did not fit into 'Darwin's theory' which was adopted approximately 200 years ago. Is this a case of inconvenient academic truth?

It is also dismissed as a theory by academia to consider the idea that ancient man knew more than contemporary man. In my opinion, this is nothing more than 'academic arrogance'. Can a contemporary theory be more accurate than an eye witness account of an actual event?

The Mayan Calendar is based upon the lunar and celestial cycles. The calendar itself has a 260 day cycle, which is quite interesting in that it correlates with the gestation period of a human; approximately nine months. The last cycle of the Mayan calendar (13 Baktun Cycles) began in 3114 BC and ended in December 2012.

The Mayan doctrines are also well-adjusted with the Egyptian pyramid code and the Hindu world age doctrine. Again, this is mostly rejected by Western scientist and authorities since it does not line up well with the established chronology of humanity.

Just like the cycles of birth, growth, and death, the 26,000 year cycle is defined by four distinct ages. The first is the 'Golden Age' which signifies enlightenment. Next is the 'Silver Age' and the 'Bronze Age', which shows a steady decline from the enlightenment of the Golden Age. Finally, the 'Iron Age' or 'Age of Darkness' is known for corruption, ignorance, chaos, and alienation from spiritual light. At the end of the Iron Age, the cycle begins again; beginning another Golden Age of Enlightenment.

The Mayan calendar can be broken into subparts which correspond to the Zodiac. The ancient Egyptians clearly understood the Zodiac and applied it as a method of keeping time.

Each of the 12 signs of the Zodiac has distinctive qualities and energies. There are four elements of the Zodiac. First is the 'Fire' or creative element. Next is 'Earth' or material followed by 'Air' also known as intellectual and 'Water' which symbolizes emotion. Each of the elements represent approximately 2000 years.

It is also interesting to point out that midway through the last Baktun (approximately 550 BC) humanity witnessed the emergence of great teachers, philosophers, and other people of enlightenment such as Pythagoras, Buddha, Zoroaster, etc. Is this a coincidence or did the 'primitive cultures' know something that we do not?

The Palermo Stone and the Turin Papyrus are

HISTORICAL ARTIFACTS WHICH CONTAIN AN INTERESTING CHRONOLOGY SUPPORTING A MUCH LONGER HISTORY OF HUMANITY. A LIST OF RULERS AND PERIOD OF RULE IS METICULOUSLY AND SUCCINCTLY DOCUMENTED.[9]

IF THE LIST OF RULERS, DYNASTIES, AND TIME AS A RULER IS ADDED TOGETHER, THE CALCULATION RESULTS IN A TIMELINE OF APPROXIMATELY 34,000 TO 36,000 BC. THIS IS CERTAINLY FURTHER BACK IN HISTORY THAN MODERN CONTEMPORARY EGYPTOLOGISTS HYPOTHESIZE AND REPRESENTS A BROADER TIMELINE THAN WE ARE TOLD BY THESE 'AUTHORITIES / EXPERTS'. THE DATE RANGE ALSO CORRESPONDS WITH A GOLDEN AGE OF ENLIGHTENMENT.

THE ANCIENT EGYPTIANS DID NOT BELIEVE IN PHYSICAL DEATH. THEIR ANCIENT LANGUAGE OF SOUF DOES NOT HAVE A WORD FOR DEATH. INSTEAD, THE WORD "WESTING" (FIGURATIVELY 'GOING WEST') IS USED TO REPRESENT IMMORTALITY AND REBIRTH, JUST AS THE SUN SETS IN THE WEST AND RE-APPEARS A SHORT TIME LATER IN THE EAST.

THE EGYPTIAN RITUALS MIMICKED THE CYCLES OF THE SUN AND STARS TO ARTICULATE THE CYCLE OF LIFE. "HELIACAL RISING" REPRESENTS APPROXIMATELY 70 DAYS IN WHICH A STAR DISAPPEARS INTO THE 'UNDERWORLD' AND REAPPEARS OR IS REBORN. IS THERE SOMETHING MORE TO THIS EGYPTIAN BELIEF?

THE PYRAMID CODE CONTAINS OVER 4000

---

[9] *Royal Annals of Ancient Egypt* by Wilkinson and Toby A. H. Wilkinson

Egyptian hieroglyphs.[10] The code was discovered in 1799 in Rashid when French workers uncovered the Rosetta Stone. The Rosetta Stone was in Greek and Egyptian languages and three different scripts that were used throughout the region.

Jean-François Champollion and Thomas Young deciphered the Rosetta Stone in 1822.[11] Thought to be the definitive interpretation of the code, contemporary authors such as Laird Scranton have cast doubts on the findings of Champollion and Young.

In his book, Sacred Symbols of the Dogon: The Key to Advanced Science in the Ancient Egyptian Hieroglyphs[12], Scranton provides a compelling argument for his cosmological hypothesis.

As an interesting side note, when Stephen Hawking was asked how many fundamental particles there are, he responded "over 200". When asked the same question, a Dogon priest responded "266"[13]. What secret does the reclusive tribe of Dogon in Mali know?

While Champollion and Young interpreted

---

[10] *Encyclopedia of Anthropology by H. James Birx*

[11] *Essay on Dr Young's and M. Champollion's Phonetic System of Hieroglyphics by Henry Salt*

[12] *ISBN-10: 1594771340*

[13] *Laird Scranton - The Pyramid Code (cast http://www.pyramidcode.com/Cast.html)*

the hieroglyphs and 26 letters written on the Rosetta Stone as 'individual' in meaning, Scranton's interpretation indicates the 26 letters do not carry the same meaning as our contemporary alphabet but carry individual 'concepts' and the words actually form an extended 'sentence'.

Our contemporary civilization employs the same method in communication and while this may sound confusing, it becomes easier to understand if you apply Scranton's concept using acronyms.

For instance, "USA" has a distinct meaning (United States of America) which is identifiable and fully understood by many. If you separate these letters and rely upon individual letters, the meaning does not remain the same.

Another example of Scranton's interpretation is the acronym "FYI" (For Your Information). Together, these letters add meaning for the message receiver.

Changing the currently accepted chronology for mankind is obviously a daunting task, full of pitfalls and academic quagmire and bureaucracy however, some legitimate questions beg for plausible answers. One such cosmic 'riddle' is found in the Nubian Desert.

Nabta Playa is the oldest known place of

astronomical measurement once used to track the movements of the celestial bodies across the canopy of the night sky[14]. It is a modern location for the study of archeoastronomy.

The Stellae Megaliths found at Nabta Playa point to Orion's brightest star, the rising position of Sirius, the brightest star of the Big Dipper, and the circumpolar region of the nighttime sky which the Pyramid Text refers to as "Where stars never die"; thus "Westing". The ancient civilizations were not only constructing a map of the sky, they were actually tracking the celestial movements to measure time.

The tracking of stars and planets was used to construct calendars used to signal changing seasons, such as coming monsoons. This was very important information for these nomadic tribes because what is now desert, was once a green and lush area due to this cyclical timeline.

While stones cannot be carbon dated, other artifacts found in the Nabta Playa area and surrounding basin indicate a civilization which used sacred cosmology and advanced astrology as far back in history as 10,000 BC.

While many contemporary experts dismiss the idea of ancient Nabta Playa being an oasis or

---

[14] *Pyramid Quest: Secrets of the Great Pyramid and the Dawn of Civilization* by Robert M. Schoch, Robert Aquinas McNally

AREA OF VAST WATER REFUGE HOWEVER, A COMPELLING QUESTION REMAINS: "WHY ARE SEASHELLS PRESENT THROUGHOUT THE VAST DESERT?" ONE COMPELLING HYPOTHESIS 'FITS' BETTER IN HISTORY THAN THE CURRENTLY ESTABLISHED CONVENTION. WHAT IF NABTA PLAYA WAS ONCE LOCATED ON THE RIVER NILE?

WE KNOW RIVERS HAVE AND WILL MOVE AND CHANGE COURSE OVER TIME. FROM THE NILE TO THE SUTLEJ, FROM THE HUANG HE TO THE OXBOWS OF THE MISSISSIPPI, RIVERS CONTINUE TO SNAKE ACROSS THE TOPOGRAPHY OF EVERY LANDSCAPE. THIS IS EVIDENT AROUND THE WORLD.

THE RIVER NILE HAS MOVED AS RECORDED IN HISTORY[15] HOWEVER, COULD IT HAVE MOVED APPROXIMATELY 60 MILES THROUGH THE DESERT? THE ANSWER IS "YES".

THERE ARE ALSO OTHER INDICATIONS OF THE PAST AGES FOUND IN EGYPT. NEOLITHIC CAVE DRAWINGS OF COWS, BULLS, AND SACRED CALVES WERE FOUND IN THE 'CAVE OF SWIMMERS' LOCATED IN THE GILF KEBIR PLATEAU OF THE SAHARA. THIS CAVE WAS ONCE UNDERNEATH AN ANCIENT LAKE. THESE DRAWINGS ARE REPRESENTATIVE OF THE NOMADIC 'COW CULTS' OF THE NILE VALLEY WHOSE LIVES REVOLVED AROUND THE WORSHIP OF HATHOR.

THE DRAWINGS ARE BELIEVED TO BE FROM THE

---

[15] *The Physiography of the River Nile and Its Basin by Maslahat Al-Misahah*

Taurus period (the height of the Cow Cults) during the last Egyptian Golden Age. Taurus, one of the oldest constellations, found in the Paleolithic cave art in Lascaux (France). It has been radiocarbon dated at 17,000 years old.[16]

There are also astonishing similarities between the sign of Leo and the Sphinx. The body and posture both hold the likeness of a lion. Could this influence produce a 10,000 BC artifact with such immaculate engineering and advanced construction? Is this a coincidence or something more?

History is littered with signs, symbols, and subtle messages hidden in plain sight. It is the conclusion drawn from this information that is often misinterpreted. The evidence provided herein invokes serious questions requiring reasonable and plausible answers.

My conclusion: Intelligent civilizations existed long before the timelines provided by contemporary authorities.

What is your conclusion?

---

[16] *Modern Esoteric: Beyond Our Senses* by Brad Olsen

SANCTUM OF SHADOWS · SPIRITUS OCCULTUS

SOLVE ET COAGULA

"FALSEHOOD IS INVARIABLY THE CHILD OF FEAR IN ONE FORM OR ANOTHER."

ALEISTER CROWLEY

ARGUMENT: "THE KNIGHTS TEMPLAR ORDER WAS NOT DECIMATED BY KING PHILIP IN 1307."

ON NOVEMBER 27, 1095, IN CLERMONT, FRANCE ODO LAGERY (POPE URBAN II) CALLED FOR A RISE AGAINST THE MUSLIMS IN THE EAST[17] WITH TWO OBJECTIVES: 1) BLOCK ISLAMIC GROWTH AND 2) RECLAIM JERUSALEM. THE FIRST "HOLY WAR" HAD BEEN DECLARED.

MANPOWER WAS NEEDED TO ACHIEVE VICTORY IN WHAT BECAME KNOWN AS THE "CRUSADES". BY 1096, A PROGRAM OF 'INDULGENCE' WAS INSTITUTED TO ENLIST CRIMINALS IN SUPPORT OF THE CRUSADES.

TO INCREASE THE NUMBER OF WARRIORS AND

---

[17] http://www.history.com/this-day-in-history/pope-urban-ii-orders-first-crusade

Knights, the "Passagem Generale" (anyone can go) allowed those of questionable criminal backgrounds to be forgiven any charges and debts in exchange for allegiance to the Catholic Church as soldiers. This allowed robbers, rapists, and murderers to become Knights with the full support and authority of the established Church.[18]

This was the ultimate "get out of jail" offer and this "Nobel Army" would later disembowel their victims in search of 'swallowed' gold and jewels and loot Constantinople with acts such as scratching gold leaf from the Cathedral of Hagia Sophia frescoes.[19]

As history would have it, these greedy hoards enabled the creation and meteoric rise to power of "Pauperes Commilitones Christi Templique Salomonici", also known as the Knights Templar.

The Knights Templar has been call the "Keepers of Sacred Knowledge" as well as "Devil Worshippers". The order came into existence in 1119 with Hugues de Payens (the first Templar Grand Master) and nine Templars who were related by blood or marriage.

After the fall of Jerusalem in 1099, the East

---
[18] *The Knights Templar Chronology: Tracking History's Most Intriguing Monks* by George Smart
[19] *The Hagia Sophia: The History of the Famous Church and Mosque* by Charles River Editors

was a popular destination for European travelers however, the journey could be quite treacherous. Thieves and bandits awaited along the roads and the Knights Templar was charged with escorting travelers as protectors.

The first headquarters was in "Templum Solomonis" or Solomon's Temple[20] (Al Aqsa Mosque) and from the location, the name "Templar" was derived. Shortly after moving into the temple, the Templar order began working on a project which neither improved safety along the roads nor protected travelers from dangers; they became 'excavators'.

During the next few years, the Knights Templar tunneled from their headquarters to the Temple Mount.[21] Major excavations began and continued until ending abruptly (circa) 1128. The tunnels were later discovered by the British Royal Engineers in 1867.

Many have speculated the reasons for the excavations and conspiracy theorists claim artifacts such as secret historical documents, the Cauldron of Plenty, Spear of Destiny, and Holy Grail were found by the Templar order.

The original nine Knights Templar promptly returned to the West where the Templar Order

---
[20] *The Temple of Solomon: From Ancient Israel to Secret Societies* by James Wasserman
[21] *Jerusalem's Temple Mount: From Solomon to the Golden Dome* by Hershel Shanks

BECAME WEALTHY AND VERY POWERFUL WITHIN A VERY SHORT PERIOD OF TIME.[22]

IN WOLFRAM VON ESCHENBACH'S POEM "PARZIVAL", THE TEMPELEISEN BROTHERHOOD WAS SAID TO BE THE KEEPERS OF THE HOLY GRAIL. THIS REFERENCE HAS SINCE LINKED THE KNIGHTS TEMPLAR WITH THE GRAIL, FUELING THE STORYLINE OF POPULAR BOOKS AND MOVIES SUCH AS "THE DA VINCI CODE". PERHAPS THE 'DIVINE' SECRET IS A CONCEPT THAT IS VERY FAMILIAR TO, AND EASILY UNDERSTOOD BY, MORTALS; "GREED".

THE JEWISH REVOLT OF 66 AD IS RECORDED IN HISTORY AS ONE OF THE BLOODIEST CONFLICTS BETWEEN THE JEWS AND ROMAN OCCUPIERS. ONE OF THE DEAD SEA SCROLLS FOUND IN KHIRBET QUMRAN (1952) MAY HOLD THE ANSWER.[23] REFERRED TO AS THE COPPER SCROLL, THIS WRITTEN ON COPPER INSTEAD OF PARCHMENT OR PAPYRUS.

WHAT REALLY DIFFERENTIATES THIS SCROLL FROM THE OTHERS IS THE CONTENTS; IT IS AN INVENTORY LIST OF GOLD AND SILVER. THIS TREASURE (APPROXIMATELY 200 TONS) IS THOUGHT TO HAVE BEEN BURIED BY THE JEWS DURING THE REVOLT IN 66 AD. THE LOCATION — THE JEWISH TEMPLE ON THE TEMPLE MOUNT. THIS IS INDEED AN INTERESTING 'COINCIDENCE'.

---

[22] *Knights of the Holy Grail: The Secret History of The Knights Templar by Tim Wallace-Murphy*

[23] *Methods of Investigation of the Dead Sea Scrolls and the Khirbet Qumran Site: Present Realities and Future Prospects by Norman Golb (Author), Michael Owen Wise (Editor), John J. Collins (Contributor)*

The Knights Templar returned to the West in 1129 and began recruiting, enabling the Order to grow substantially in the coming years. Along with their acquisition of power came large tracts of land and great wealth, which is interesting given the economic conditions in France at the time of their return. Where did this wealth come from? One plausible explanation that makes sense, at least to me, is strictly monetary.

From 1129 until 1150, the Knights Templar created the very first system of 'Travelers Checks' or "Chits" which were notes of currency using a code created by the Templar which served as a 'password'. This enabled the holder of the note to cash it for real currency. Without the 'password' code, the note was without any value even if stolen from the holder.

Codes were used throughout history, with Julius Caesar expanding the practice of encryption in the Roman Empire. During the 13th century, Roger Bacon began studying and developing cyphers for message encryption which enabled information "in the clear" with only the intended recipient knowing the meaning of the message.[24]

The methodology was very simple; a traveler would visit the local Knights Templar

---

[24] *The First Scientist: A Life of Roger Bacon* by Brian Clegg

commandery or "outpost" (Templar House), and produce currency, land, jewels, land deeds, or anything else of collateral value.[25] It would be taken by the Templar and a chit would be issued with an encrypted code, providing the value of the note.

The traveler would make the journey and visit the Templar outpost at the destination. There he / she would produce the chit, it would be decrypted and currency would be issued for the amount. This was such a success, the traveler check system is still used today.

Another method of 'credit card' was used for currency during the journey. Collateral was provided at the Templar outpost and an encrypted chit was issued. Along the route to the destination, the traveler could used the chit to purchase supplies and lodging at a Templar outpost. Upon arrival at the destination, the traveler would produce the chit and the balance (credit or debit) would be refunded or collected.

Obviously, these systems were lucrative for the Knights Templar. Although "usury" was not permitted, "rent" was allowed and so the Templar simply "rented" to lodging, currency, etc., to the traveler. This was a creative was to side-step

---

[25] *History of the Knights Templar Paperback by Charles G Addison (Author), C G Addison (Author), David Hatcher Childress (Author, Introduction), First Last (Author)*

the prohibition and still collect 'interest'.[26]

Another contributing factor to the success of the Knights Templar was the Omne Datum Optimum, a papal bull issued by Pope Innocent II in 1139. This was a formal approval and endorsement for the Templar which also validated the Order.

> "As for the things that you will receive from the spoils, you can confidently put them to your own use, and we prohibit that you be coerced against your will to give anyone a portion of these."[27]
>
> Omne Datum Optimum 1139

The "Milites Templi" (1144) and "Militia Dei" (1145), were papal bulls which provided additional rights and privileges for the Knights Templar including fiduciary rights such as freedom to cross borders, tax exempt status, collection of taxes, tithes, and burial fees. Along with the Omne Datum Optimum and the seemingly divine intervention enabling (against all odds) Saladin's defeat at Montgisard

---

[26] *Knights of the Holy Grail: The Secret History of The Knights Templar by Tim Wallace-Murphy*

[27] *https://en.wikipedia.org/wiki/Omne_Datum_Optimum*

(1177),[28] the foundation had been built upon which the Templar would achieve new heights of success.

As a result, the Templar became a "secret" order and began moving into other financial ventures; import and export, factories, landlords, banking and loans, businesses supporting the efforts in the East, and even building a fleet of ships which were sailed to the East. The Port of La Rochelle was constructed as the base of operations while the ships were in France.

Equal too, would be the descent into the precipice for the future Templar. Ten years after Saladin's defeat at Montgisard, the 1187 Battle of Hattin, also known as the "Battle of the Horns of Hattin", began a series of events which would lead to the ultimate demise of the Knights Templar Order.

Under the command of the Grand Master of the Templar, Gerard de Ridefort, the mounting arrogance of the Order (especially Ridefort's) caused an implosion resulting in a total defeat of the Knights Templar forces.

Ridefort, due to political influences, inner turmoil, arrogance, and stubbornness, chose to pursue Saladin's superior numbered forces,

---

[28] *Medieval Warfare: A History by Maurice Keen*

including Hashishin (users of hashish) assassins, into the desert during mid-day heat.

Against advisement, Ridefort attacked Saladin and suffered a crippling defeat which resulted in the execution of the Templar prisoners and capture of Ridefort (et al). This paved the way for Saladin to conquer Jerusalem later in 1187.

On Friday, October 13th, 1307, the Knights Templar luck changed forever. King Philip the Fair (Philip le Bel) of France, ordered the arrest of all Knights Templar and seizure of their possessions.[29] They were charged with capital offenses ranging from worshiping Baphomet, practicing Witchcraft and Devil worship, committing unholy 'crucifix perversions', and worshipping a severed head.

Interestingly, at the time of the arrest warrant, King Philip IV was deep in debt to the Templar Order[30] and as a side note, Dante Alighieri began writing his "Divina Commedia" (The Divine Comedy) during the same year.

Petitions from Jacques de Molay (Grand Master of the Knights Templar) to Pope Clement

---

[29] *History of the Knights Templar Paperback by Charles G Addison (Author), C G Addison (Author), David Hatcher Childress (Author, Introduction), First Last (Author)*

[30] *The Warriors and the Bankers: A History of the Knights Templar from 1307 to the Present by Alan Butler (Author), Stephen Dafoe (Author)*

V (Bertrand de Got) were of no use since the Pope was firmly under the control of King Philip, who forced the papacy to move from Rome to France to ensure a greater span of control.

Pope Clement issued the papal bull named "Pastoralis Praeeminentiae" which encouraged monarchs across Europe to arrest members of the Order.

Knights Templar prisoners were turned over to the Inquisitors who successfully extracted (tortured) confessions from the accused. Many were subjected to 'Peine Forte et Dure', the Strappado, burning, beating, suffocating, the rack, the pendulum, the stocks, water torture, the Heretics Fork, the Garrote, and other forms of torture.[31] It must have seemed like a living

---

[31] *The Knights Templar: The History and Myths of the Legendary Military Order* by Sean Martin

'Malebolge on Earth' for those poor victims.

In 1312, the "Vox in excelso" papal bull dissolved the Knights Templar.

"….We subject it to perpetual prohibition with the approval of the Holy Council, strictly forbidding anyone to presume to enter the said order in the future, or to receive or wear its habit, or to act as a Templar."[32]

Vox in excelso

The "Ad providam" followed the "Vox in excelso" and ordered the Templar assets to be distributed to eight geographical divisions (langue) by the Knights Hospitaller Fraternitas Hospitalaria; the Knights Hospitaller.

During this year, the estimated 15,000 Templar outposts (houses) were liquidated. And so, this ended the Knights Templar order forever…..or did it really?

The Knights Templar arrest warrants were dated September 14, 1307, which provided approximately four weeks of advanced warning that the arrests were planned for October 13,

---

[32] https://en.wikipedia.org/wiki/Vox_in_excelso

1307.[33] There is no evidence this information was limited to an immediate "need to know status" since the warrants were processed in normal due course.

The 'Rule of the Templar Order' commanded the Order members to defend one another, even until death.[34] With the Order being firmly entrenched within the society, there is no reason to believe the arrest warrants were secret. Perhaps this was done intentionally; knowingly leaking the information while maintaining 'plausible deniability'.

It is widely believed that only 1/10 of the Order was ultimately arrested; approximately 600 individual Templars.[35] Is this because the King's agents could only find 600 members of the Order? Certainly, with over 15,000 outposts (houses) existing on the morning of October 13, 1307, more than 600 could have been arrested.

Another interesting point is that the King's agents who made the arrests and conducted the searches of the Templar dwellings found very little 'wealth' and the immaculate documents and records kept by the Order had mysteriously vanished.

---

[33] *The Warriors and the Bankers: A History of the Knights Templar from 1307 to the Present* by Alan Butler (Author), Stephen Dafoe (Author)

[34] *The Rule of the Templars (Studies in the History of Medieval Religion)* by J.M. Upton-Ward

[35] *Knights of the Holy Grail: The Secret History of The Knights Templar* by Tim Wallace-Murphy

According to the testimony of Knights Templar Jean de Châlon, the Order had been warned of the coming arrests and many successfully fled by land and sea with the majority of the Templar wealth.

"....... Learning beforehand about this trouble, the leaders of the Order fled, and he himself met Brother Gerard de Villiers leading fifty horses; and he heard it said that he set out to sea with eighteen galleys and that Brother Hugues de Châlons fled with the whole treasure of Brother Hugues de Pairaud."

Testimony of Jean de Châlons

Theories abound concerning the ships which mysteriously vanished from the Port of La Rochelle however, if the Templar Order wanted to sail beyond the Mediterranean Sea, it was certainly plausible.

Many knights were Normans, who have been thought of as being from French descent however, Normans were actually descendants of the 'North'; Scandinavia. These "Norsemen" were excellent sailors, able and willing to sail anywhere, including the established Viking routes across the Atlantic Ocean.

Robert the Bruce had been excommunicated which was certainly inviting for members of the Templar Order. During the 1314 Battle of Bannockburn (Blàr Allt Nam Bànag), the Knights Templar is believed to have been fighting with Robert the Bruce to defeat the superior English forces.[36]

Later in 1546, the Queen of Scots, Mary of Guise, wrote a letter to William St. Clair of France. In the letter, she wrote:

> "Likewise that we shall be loyal and a true Mistress to him, his Council and the Secret shown to us, which we shall keep secret." [sic]
>
> Mary of Guise

Many have speculated as to what the "secret" was and where the secret actually resided. Some say Rosslyn Chapel is the resting place for important artifact(s) while others claim the scriptorium in Rosslyn Castle (perhaps underneath) the structure.

Sir William St Clair, a Knight Templar, had built Rosslyn Chapel as a blueprint of Templum Solomonis" (Solomon's Temple), complete with underground tunnels and clandestine passages

---

[36] *The Knights Templar and Scotland* by Robert Ferguson

and rooms. It is said to be an exact replica of King Herod's Temple.

Sir William St Clair was also instrumental in the formation of the Freemasons and Rosslyn Chapel contains the oldest known document of a Masonic First Degree Ceremony, also known as the "Entered Apprentice".[37]

The Knights Templar had also established trade routes to the East which supported their import and export businesses throughout Europe. Some of the routes utilized the mountain passes through the Swiss Alps.

SILENCE

On November 15, 1315, three Swiss regions (approximately 1500 peasants without military experience) gathered to fight the forces of Duke Leopold I of Austria (approximately 3000 soldiers) near the Morgarten Pass in Switzerland. These peasants, supported by eye-witness accounts of "White Knights" defeated the Austrian forces. The three regions formed the core of modern Switzerland.[38]

---

[37] *Digest of Masonic Law of Florida F. & A.M., Chaspter 37: Initiation and Advancement*

[38] *Knights Templar: Their History and Myths Revealed by Alan Butler*

Interestingly enough, the original flag of the Old Swiss Confederacy, having a white cross which reached the edge of the banner, was an almost mirror image of the Knights Templar white flag with a red cross. Coincidence?

Many groups and organizations were formed and grew substantially in the coming years. The Rosicrucian Enlightenment, Mystery Schools, Knights of Christ, Priory of Sion, Jacobinians, Freemasons, Club of Rome, Illuminati, Scottish Rite, York Rite, Ancient Order of Druids, etc. flourished and many believe the Templar Order, having been persecuted, joined these organizations with one objective: hide in plain sight.

My conclusion: The Knights Templar Order was not decimated by King Philip in 1307. My conclusion is based upon:

A secret order with secretive pathology;
An established bond of brotherhood;
Banking / financial knowledge and expertise;
Possessing money and means to 'disappear';
Extensive use of codes, symbols, and cyphers;
Being battle-hardened warriors;
Being motivated to hide in plain sight.

To me, this is more than coincidence or

HAPPENSTANCE. I ALSO BELIEVE THE MEMBERS THAT WERE CAPTURED MADE THE ULTIMATE SACRIFICE FOR THE BROTHERHOOD.

IF JACQUES DE MOLAY HAD FLED OR NOT OBEYED KING PHILIP'S SUMMONS, THE ENSUING PURSUIT WOULD SURELY HAVE RESULTED IN MANY MORE MEMBERS OF THE ORDER SUFFERING AND BEING MURDERED BY THE CHURCH.

WHAT IS YOUR CONCLUSION?

SANCTUM OF SHADOWS · SPIRITUS OCCULTUS

PARS II - SPIRITUS INFERNUM

"As the ceremony is opened, you should pay close attention to vibrations, sounds, temperature changes, etc. Some demons manifest as slight changes in ambient lighting produced by candlelight. Others will bring an uneasy "chill" to the otherwise temperate conditions of the sanctum.

I have experienced the movement of small objects caused by a quick puff of air from an undetermined direction. These are all examples however, none are constantly present. Demons are individuals (as we) and they make their entrance as they wish."

Aleister Nacht

Argument: "The spirit world influences physical human actions."

A. NOLA

Many people believe spirits influence the living. The established religions believe and worship those spirits who will not "remain dead". From early days, humans have searched for reasons and justifications for good and bad events which impacted their lives.

It is easy to see human linear thinking and draw the same conclusions, from an adverse event to humans blaming some unseen spirit for their particular situation or plight, from one perspective to another. Established religion actually supports the idea of spirits, including the Christian 'Nicene Creed'.

> "He [Jesus] was crucified for us under Pontius Pilate; he suffered and was buried. The third day he rose again, according to the Scriptures."

This not only represents the rising of the dead, but in the Bible, the stated consumption of the flesh.

Jesus said to them, "Very truly I tell you, unless you eat the flesh of the Son of Man and drink his blood, you have no life in you.

Many experts support the notion that spirits are nothing more than a psychological premonition or imagination, which humans can actually believe they see. It is quite common for those who have had a traumatic experience to report some type of paranormal activity concurrently occurring with the actual event.

While this can be neither proven nor disproven with scientific methods, there are documented cases by clinical experts which reveal something unseen has in fact occurred. The skeptics, especially atheists, argue that all of these perceptions are simply parlor tricks or only in the mind of the person reporting the event.

One fact is true; people are influenced by "something or someone" as evidenced by inhuman brutality toward one another. Whether this is demonic possession or simply a natural action, the question remains: "Are these individuals truly influenced by external forces or acting of their own volition"?

One such case that merits closer examination took place during August of 2005 in New Orleans (aka La Nouvelle-Orléans), Louisiana. In the aftermath of Hurricane Katrina, there were many instances of the horrors witnessed which could certainly be comparable to war time and the inconceivable events which happen during war.

This occurrence in the French Quarter (aka Vieux Carré) caused the death of Addie Hall who had decided to remain in New Orleans although the Louisiana Governor had issued an evacuation order. Addie and her boyfriend, Zack Bowen, lived in the French Quarter and instead of evacuation chose to remain behind and "ride out" the storm with a few neighbors and friends as the storm ravaged Southern Louisiana.

The two lived in an apartment at 826 North Rampart Street above a voodoo shop and some believe a source of negative energy and restless, angry spirits. No one knows for sure exactly what happened during those weeks as the two were sequestered due to the rising water level. One thing is true; the two ended up dead.

Police were called to the Omni Hotel in the French Quarter where Bowen had in fact committed suicide by jumping from the roof to his death. When police officers responded, they found a note and Bowen's dog tags from his service in the military.

According to the note, Bowen had jumped from the roof in order to end his pain and suffering for certain events, including the murder of his girlfriend Addie Hall. Along with this was the contact information for his landlord who would ultimately respond with police to open the door to Bowen and Hall's apartment.

Once entering the apartment, police found a grizzly spectacle. Police found Addie's body parts and torso in the refrigerator. They also found her head in a pot on the stove which had been boiled to the point that the flash was falling from the bone.

Police also uncovered parts of Addie in the oven, having been baked for such a long period of time as to render it chard. While investigating the events, it was noticed that Zack had written things on the wall alluding to events and ultimately the murder of Addie.

Those who knew Zach Bowen reported he was a mild mannered person, personable, and helpful to others. His profession was that of a bartender and he and Addie both worked as a bartender in the French Quarter. It was also reported that Addie was a dancer in some of the local burlesque and strip club establishments off of Bourbon Street.

The two became close friends and ultimately moved beyond friendship and acquired an apartment together before Hurricane Katrina. The two were reported to be quiet neighbors and were always willing to invite someone for a drink. There was also a darker side.

Addie had a very short temper and her temper would erupt almost without provocation and many times Zack was the point of her hostility. There is evidence to prove the police were called and responded several times to domestic disturbances between the two. While some of these responses are dismissed as drunken "fun", (such as Addie flashing her breasts to responding police officers) other times there were actually fist fights and Addie had hit Zack numerous times in the face, head, and neck. These were not "love taps" but blood drawing events which were serious in nature.

It is unknown if Addie's temper and the hostilities between the two escalated in the weeks after Katrina's arrival. One thing is for certain; Zack murdered, dismembered and ultimately cooked Addie's remains.

KATRINA

Many people speculate as to how a mild

mannered person could end up going over the edge resulting in such extreme actions. No one will ever know for sure however, experts like Alyne Pustanio[39] speculate that Zack was in fact possessed by a demonic spirits.

New Orleans is a rich culture of modern practices and historical magic. It is one of the oldest cities for Voudon, voodoo, Hoodoo, and other magical practices in the United States. Voodoo invites spirits to enter into the host, allow The host to gain (and understand) supernatural knowledge, and foresee the future.

Some speculate that the spirits were too powerful and being in such close proximity to Bowen and hall, spirits were able to overcome the two and manifest as spirit possession.

In his book <u>An Exorcist Tells His Story</u>[40], Gabriele Amorth discusses the topic of exorcism and provides the following narratives for clarification and understanding of demonic activities.

<u>Demonic Possession</u> - "This occurs when Satan takes full possession of the body (not the soul); he speaks and acts without the knowledge or

---

[39] https://www.amazon.com/Alyne-A-Pustanio/e/B00W0BHQ7M

[40] https://www.amazon.com/gp/product/0898707102/

consent of the victim, who therefore is morally blameless."

<u>Diabolical Oppression</u> - "There is no possession, loss of consciousness, or involuntary action and word."

<u>Diabolic Obsession</u> - "Symptoms include sudden attacks, at times ongoing, of obsessive thoughts, sometimes even rationally absurd, but of such nature that the victim is unable to free himself."

<u>Diabolic Infestation</u> - "Infestations affect houses, things, or animals."

<u>Diabolical Subjugation</u> - "People fall into this form of evil when thy voluntarily submit to Satan. The two most common forms of dependence are the blood pact with the devil and the consecration to Satan."

During the days before Hurricane Katrina, many people evacuated New Orleans which not only left the city in a state of emergency, but also reduce the overall population to a handful of those who remained. For this reason, the spirits in and around New Orleans (including aboveground Native American burials and vast graveyards) simply possessed those predisposed individuals who remained in New Orleans.

After Hurricane Katrina ravaged Louisiana, eighty percent of New Orleans was under water, creating an 'island effect' in the French Quarter, which is five feet above sea level.[41] This isolated Vieux Carré from the rest of New Orleans.

With the abundance of death, dead bodies in the streets, the smell of death everywhere, and the horrific events afterword certainly these spirits would be able to manifest (without conjure) and occupy areas of the fallen city and ultimately, possess certain individuals who were pre-disposed to such activities.

Zack Bowen had experience mental illness issues earlier in life, beginning with his service and ultimate discharge from the military. Zach had been deployed and fought around Baghdad and the surrounding areas in Iraq. One source reports that Zack's close friend was killed in combat and after that event Zack began a journey down a road of seclusion, mistrust, and unstable personality.

Since Zach received a general discharge, he was denied medical services (including possible

---

[41] https://en.wikipedia.org/wiki/French_Quarter

PSYCHIATRIC CARE) AFTER LEAVING THE MILITARY. WHETHER THIS HAD ANY BEARING ON THE MURDER AND SUICIDE IS UNKNOWN HOWEVER, ONE THING IS FOR CERTAIN: ZACK WAS MENTALLY 'ON-HIS-OWN'. WITHOUT THE SUPPORT OF MEDICAL SERVICES, ZACK WOULD HAVE BEEN PRIMED FOR THE ROLE WHICH ULTIMATELY LED TO HIS OWN DEMISE.

SO, WAS THIS AN INSTANCE OF DEMONIC POSSESSION RESULTING FROM 1) ZACK'S PREDISPOSITION TO MENTAL ILLNESS; 2) HIS CLOSE PROXIMITY TO THE VOODOO SHOP BELOW HIS APARTMENT; 3) THE PENT-UP FRUSTRATION AND HEARTACHE RESULTING FROM THE LOSS OF A CLOSE FRIEND IN IRAQ? TRULY, WE MAY NEVER KNOW.

B. PENNSYLVANIA DUTCH POWWOWING

IN 1820, JOHN GEORGE HOHMAN'S BOOK CALLED "THE LONG LOST FRIEND"[42] WAS PUBLISHED. THE BOOK (REFERRED TO AS A 'MANUAL' BY SOME) IS A COLLECTION OF FOLK MAGIC REMEDIES, MAGICAL SPELLS, TALISMANS, MYSTICISM, AND GNOSIS USED FOR HEALING AND THE TRADITION OF 'POW-WOW'.

POW-WOW, WHICH COMBINES TRADITIONAL REMEDIES, FAITH HEALING AND FOLK MAGIC ORIGINATED IN THE PENNSYLVANIA DUTCH COMMUNITY. FOREMOST POW-WOW PRACTITIONER

---

[42] *German translation: Der lang vermisste Freund*

EXPLAINS THE ORIGIN:

> "IT [POW-WOW] WAS DEVELOPED DURING A TIME OF SUPERSTITION AND LITTLE SCIENTIFIC UNDERSTANDING... BUT ALSO A TIME OF DEEP FAITH COUPLED WITH FEAR OF THE UNKNOWN."[43]

NELSON REHMEYER, A POW-WOW "DOCTOR" (PRACTITIONER), LIVED IN SHREWSBURY, LOCATED IN SOUTH-CENTRAL PENNSYLVANIA. HE WAS A GENTLE AND AMICABLE PERSON AS DESCRIBED BY THOSE WHO KNOW HIM. NO EVIDENCE EXISTS WHICH INDICATES REHMEYER PRACTICED SCHWARZE MAGIE (BLACK MAGIC) OR "HEXED"[44] ANYONE. HIS MURDER IN 1928 WOULD PLACE POWWOWING AND THE PENNSYLVANIA DUTCH COMMUNITY IN THE MEDIA SPOTLIGHT.

REHMEYER WAS MURDERED BY JOHN BLYMIRE, WHO ALSO CLAIMED TO BE A "POWWOWER", BELIEVED REHMEYER HAD PLACED A HEX ON HIM. THIS IDEA WAS FUELED BY A LOCAL PRACTICING WITCH BY THE NAME OF NELLIE NOLL (AKA WITCH OF MARIETTA).

KNOPP HAD TOLD BLYMIRE HE WOULD NEED REHMEYER'S SPELL BOOK OR LOCK OF HAIR IN ORDER TO LIFT THE CURSE AND SO BLYMIRE, ALONG WITH ACQUAINTANCES WILBERT HESS AND JOHN CURRY,

---

[43] Robert Phoenix: http://braucher.webs.com/frequentquestions.htm

[44] "Hexerei" is the study of Witchcraft according to the Pennsylvania Dutch

went to Rehmeyer's house to do just that. The events which occurred in Rehmeyer's Hollow seem to be related to phantomic shedim[45] instead of outright audible enticements. It was speculated that Blymire also unsuccessfully attempted to telepathically "will" Rehmeyer to surrender his spell book.[46]

When Rehmeyer uncooperatively resisted their demands, the three beat and burned him to death which, according to Blymire, achieved the same objective of breaking the hex. Later asked for the motivation for the crime, John Blymire showed no remorse and was relieved that Rehmeyer's hex died with him that night; claiming self defense was his only option.

In this tangled web of magic, a man lost his life due to a very strong belief in evil and hexes. Whether real or perceived by imagination, John Blymire's actions were a direct result of the unseen spiritual world.

C. Spectral Evidence

"Although the plantation supported his merchant ventures, Parris was dissatisfied with his lack of financial security and began to look

---

[45] *A Jewish Shedim demon seduces humanity with learning, knowledge, and power.*

[46] *Crime Buff's Guide to Outlaw Pennsylvania by Ron Franscell, and Karen Valentine*

TO THE MINISTRY.[47]"

In 1692, Samuel Parris' daughter, Elizabeth "Betty" Parris, and her cousin Abigail Williams accused Parris' slave Tituba of witchcraft. This event set the stage for a frenzy of blood-lust in the small town of Salem Village in Massachusetts. Before the accusations and witch trials had ended, approximately 72 people were accused and tried, 19 persons and two dogs were hanged, and one was "pressed to death"[48].

Spectral evidence was key proof delivered against the accused Salem witches in 1692. Spectral evidence refers to a witness testimony that the accused person's spirit or spectral shape appeared to him/her witness in a dream at the time the accused person's physical body was at another location.[49]

While the Salem Witch Trials introduced the 'New World' to Spectral Evidence, it had already been used years earlier in England. It was introduced as a secular statute during the reign of Queen Elizabeth I in 1558. The statute stated that all who, "use, practice, or exercise any witchcraft, enchantment, charm or sorcery,

---

[47] *https://en.wikipedia.org/wiki/Samuel_Parris*

[48] *Peine forte et dure (described as crushing)*

[49] *https://definitions.uslegal.com/s/spectral-evidence/*

WHEREBY ANY PERSON SHALL HAPPEN TO BE KILLED OR DESTROYED...SHALL SUFFER PAINS OF DEATH."[50]

UNFORTUNATELY, THE STATUTE REMAINED SILENT ON WHAT EVIDENCE COULD OR COULD NOT BE ADMITTED AT TRIAL. THE USE OF SPECTRAL EVIDENCE IN ENGLAND BECAME MORE COMMON DURING THE REIGN OF CHARLES II AND JAMES II.

IN SALEM, MAGISTRATES JOHN HATHORNE AND JONATHAN CORWIN HELD HEARINGS TO GATHER TESTIMONY AGAINST THOSE ACCUSED OF WITCHCRAFT. INTERESTINGLY ENOUGH, CORWIN'S MOTHER-IN-LAW WAS ACCUSED OF WITCHCRAFT BY HER SERVANT HOWEVER, WAS NEVER CHARGED.

SOME SPECULATION EXISTS CONCERNING THE INITIAL CAUSE OF THE WITCH TRIALS HOWEVER, THERE IS NO QUESTION AS TO THE GREED INVOLVED AS A SUSTAINING FORCE AND BYPRODUCT OF THE PROCESS. IF AN ACCUSED PERSON CONFESSED, HE OR SHE WOULD LOSE THEIR PROPERTY TO THE CHURCH. FOR THIS REASON, LANDOWNERS WERE USUALLY THE PROMINENT INDIVIDUALS ACCUSED OF WITCHCRAFT AND THE MAJORITY WERE CONVICTED (OR CONFESSED) DUE TO A 'PREPONDERANCE' OF SPECTRAL EVIDENCE. THIS SEEMS LIKE "CERCA TROVA" WITHOUT EVIDENCE.

IN SOME CASES, SUCH AS GILES CORY, THE MOTIVE SEEM TO BE MORE DRIVEN BY GREED THAN THE PURITAN BELIEFS. GILES CORY WAS ARRESTED AND

---

[50] *Notestein, A History of Witchcraft in England, 14.*

accused of witchcraft. When asked for his plea, he refused to plead guilty or not guilty.

Because of his refusal to plead, Cory was led to a pit where boards were placed on his chest and on the boards, heavy stones were placed. This torture method[51] was designed to extract a plea from the victim. Since Cory was a land and livestock owner, his estate would be very lucrative to the church. As with most cases, the victim's possessions were given to the church after the trial.

In Corey's case however, he had taken action and changed his will before the accusation. All his possessions passed to his two son-in-laws in accordance with his will. Cory never pleaded nor confessed during his ordeal. Before his death, he cursed the town of Salem. His last words are said to have been "More weight".

Bridget Bishop owned an apple orchard, which was located at what is now 43 Church Street and lived in a house somewhere near the orchard. She also sold cider manufactured from apples grown in her orchard.[52] She was the first victim, hanged in her apple orchard.

In 1692, the Superior Court of Judicature was created and heard the last twenty-six cases

---

[51] *Peine forte et dure*

[52] *Boyer, p. 192.*

PENDING AGAINST THE ACCUSED. THE NEW COURT IGNORED SPECTRAL EVIDENCE AND TWENTY-THREE WERE FOUND NOT GUILTY AND THREE WERE PARDONED BY THE GOVERNOR, THUS ENDING THE WITCH TRIALS.

ONE QUESTION REMAINS: "WHO WAS MORE EVIL; THE ACCUSED OR THE ACCUSERS?" WHAT IS YOUR CONCLUSION?

Sathanas Nos Liberavit

There are certain aspects to the parallax dimension and the thin veil that separates our human reality from celestial reality. As with all things human, there is always the possibility the truth is well beyond human comprehension.

It is always funny to listen to those who speak from a position of authority and yet cannot solve a simple problem such as curing cancer. For this reason, we are limited in our human bodies; a flesh and bone prison in which we all exist.

In order to free the mind from the body it must be exercised. As with any task, it takes many hours of perfecting to achieve the objective. It is time consuming and tedious. We as humans only know (and will only ever know) what we have experienced through one of our five senses. For this reason we are cosmically limited and we find ourselves at a disadvantage when it comes to cognitive abilities of celestial perceptions. Although we cannot see the magnetic forces of a magnet, it does not mean the magnet will not attract metal.

Adopting this type of thought perspective is paramount for the Satanist to master, simply because there are things that cannot be seen with human (limited) eyes. Those who cry for "proof" are often those who are fooled when false proof is synthetically created simply to fulfill their need for easy answers. People want to see what is on the other side the realm however, it is not possible in some aspects of the human life due to this limitation.

The unwise, unexperienced, or unknowledgeable person who must have documented evidence that something has occurred will find that many experiences and many varying perceptions will continue to escape the eyes of the perspective beholder. It will be those who look 'outside the flesh and bone confines' who will be successful in that endeavor.

When the first humans looked at the sky and wondered what was on the other side of the stars, it began somewhat of a tradition which followed generation after generation. Modern humans still gaze at the sky in awe.

We are three dimensional creatures and anything beyond these three dimensions cannot be perceived without knowledge and practice. Magick provides both 1) attributes which enables the transition (transversal) and 2) the mechanisms which sustains the perception.

Exploration is hardwired into the human

DNA. We want to see what is behind the curtain; we want to know the reasons and explanations for occurrences and have the ability to exploit the potentials without limitations. This is a two-edged sword and for most of us, it is an irresistible force which draws us into a web of possibilities.

From the beginner to the advanced practitioner, Magick always provides the stimulus which facilitates the opening of the third eye to enable the celestial-level of conscientiousness. When the peaks are successfully scaled by a practitioner, there remains another climb just ahead. This "challenge-acceptance" methodology is actually a self-fulfilling journey of which there is neither an end nor loss of personal interest and engagement.

By subtle, yet overwhelming means, this cycle of mystery and revelation provides the cognitive exercise needed in order to become proficient at our chosen magical crafts.

We are searchers nearing our overall objective however, each layer of Magick reveals yet another mindscape, complete with its own set of challenges and rewards. Without the warm blanket of our practice to protect us from the pitfalls and complex quagmires associated with our respective magical journey, certainly we would be lost and unable to emerge from the confines of our three human dimensions.

We are often forced to placate (externally) to those who lack the cognitive ability to comprehend the very topic of the parallax dimension. It is an exhaustive pain-in-the-ass. The truth is, there are very few individuals who are reading this who can truly grasp the words written herein.

In fact, the Atheistic Satanist (which is certainly an oxymoron) reading this will quickly dismiss my attestation. For it is impossible for some to convince they are shortchanging themselves by taking the easy way out of the complex question of magick. For them, it is easier to simply say "There is nothing on the other side…..in fact, there is no other side".

These individuals have succeeded at limiting their own reality and ultimately, the reality of those who are sincerely searching for truth. This results in the 'blind leading the blind' and both are destined to fall into the chasm of the dolt, mundane imbecile.

As humans, we will only know what we have experienced. If those experiences are severely limited by circumstance or external influences,

The individual's boundaries have been summarily drawn. These boundaries limit the field of view and the ability to process abstract concepts of which magick is conceptually based.

As a direct result, these individuals experience emotional numbing and constantly struggle with creativity. The persistent internal fight with imaginary constraints and unintuitive justification of others' beliefs results in mental fatigue and physical ailments as a byproduct.

If a person surrounds themselves with lies, before long, the lies become their spacial reality which blocks the free flow of valid and plausible information.

If the neuosensors are subjected to the same bombarding inputs, those sensors become immune to any stimuli. This results in an absence of the normal highs and lows which make life interesting and worth living. If a person believes he / she knows all there is to know with such finality, any possibility of "anything more" is quickly dismissed before other difficult questions begin to surface.

We have all experienced the neanderthal who quickly attacks our theories and experiences in the virtual realm. For them, it is easier to engage in confrontation instead of intelligent

DISCUSSION. THOSE WHO THINK THEY KNOW EVERYTHING WILL NEVER UNDERSTAND ANYTHING.

THERE IS SO MUCH WE DO NOT KNOW ABOUT OUR OWN ENVIRONMENT AND OUR OWN PLANET. UNDERNEATH THE DEEPEST WATERS OF THE OCEANS THERE IS AN ENTIRE UNIVERSE OF WHICH WE KNOW VERY LITTLE.

DR. RICHARD GALLAGHER, PSYCHIATRIST AND A PROFESSOR OF CLINICAL PSYCHIATRY AT NEW YORK MEDICAL COLLEGE, IS A CONSULTANT TO THE CATHOLIC CHURCH ON MATTERS OF POSSESSION. DR. GALLAGHER PROFESSES TO HAVE WITNESSED 14 OR 15 TRUE CASES OF POSSESSION OF THE THOUSANDS HE HAS EVALUATED[53]. THERE ARE MANY PROFESSIONALS WHO WILL ATTEST THAT THERE IS IN FACT MORE JUST OUTSIDE THE REALM OF UNDERSTANDING FOR HUMANS.

---

[53] https://www.washingtonpost.com/posteverything/wp/2016/07/01/as-a-psychiatrist-i-diagnose-mental-illness-and-sometimes-demonic-possession/?utm_term=.dd3fa9e97629

IMMORTUI

There are many stories and legends from around the world that contain elements of the spirit world and the "undead". For example, zombies are not an American invention; far from it. In fact, the first recorded zombies came from China.

The Chinese believed that an improperly prepared body buried without bindings, bonds, or being securely locked in the final resting place would create what is called the Jiang Shi, a Chinese vampire / zombie.

The Arabs describe a female demon (also a prostitute) which runs throughout the desolate desert wasteland calling for her next victim. These beings are referred to as Ghouls in Persian mythology.

The Draugr comes from the Scandinavian culture of Nordic warriors of Skyrim. It is an unstoppable savage zombie which literally means the "again-walker" or "corpse at the door". It was believed that carrying the corpse out of the residence with its feet carried out first would prevent the Draugr from returning to its home. This would prevent the dead from seeing the door. Thus, the term "feet-first" was born.

From England, we have stories of the

"HUNGRY DEAD"; ALSO KNOWN AS A "REVENANT". THE REVENANT WAS FIRST DOCUMENTED BY WILLIAM OF NEWBURGH. THIS IS ZOMBIE LIKE CREATURE WOULD ROAM THE COUNTRYSIDE OF ENGLAND SEARCHING FOR A HUMAN TO CONSUME.

THE WENDIGO (CANNIBAL SPIRIT) ALGONQUIAN MYTH WAS A CANNIBALISTIC SPIRIT FOREST CREATURE THOUGHT TO TURN A LIVING CANNIBAL INTO A ZOMBIE AFTER DEATH. THE WENDIGO MENTAL ILLNESSES DISORDER EVEN HAS ITS OWN MEDICAL TITLE CALLED "WENDIGO PSYCHOSIS"[54]. SOME BELIEVE JEFFREY DAHMER (THE MILWAUKEE CANNIBAL) HAD THE DISORDER, WHICH CAUSED HIS INSATIABLE CRAVING.

THE GREEK MASCHALISMOS WOULD MUTILATE A DEAD BODY, RENDERING IT INCAPABLE OF RISING IN HOPES THAT IT WOULD NOT RETURN TO THE DOMAIN OF THE LIVING. THE "BAD DEATH" WAS THOUGHT TO TRAP A PERSON ON THIS SIDE OF THE VEIL AND THEREFORE HOLD THAT SO HOSTAGE IN A BALANCE BETWEEN THE LAND OF THE LIVING IN THE LAND OF THE DEAD.

THE GOLEM IS A JEWISH MYSTICAL CREATURE THAT TEACHES HUMANITY THE LESSON OF HUBRIS AND WARNS AGAINST THE "GOD SYNDROME". IT IS THOUGHT THAT THE GOLEM ALSO HEAVILY INFLUENCED WRITERS AND CREATORS OF FRANKENSTEIN, ZOMBIES, ETC.

GERMANIC TRIBES WHO MADE NOMADIC JOURNEYS TO THE WEST OF EUROPE BROUGHT THESE TALES OF THE

---

[54] https://en.wikipedia.org/wiki/Wendigo#Wendigo_psychosis

undead with them on their journey. These Germanic tribes were called Visigoths; who we know today as Gothic or "Goths".

Some of these myths and ancient stories evolved from true events. One such event is the "Black Death" (plague) which consumed Europe. However, there is another explanation as well. Kuru is a rare and incurable infection that can be passed from one person to another, almost like the plague.

Kuru is an early form of 'mad cow disease' affecting the people of Papua New Guinea. This disease was contracted by eating contaminated human brain tissue[55]. Once contracted, prions (proteins) eat the brains from the inside causing the host to become almost zombie-like in nature. These prions continue to eat the subjects brains until there is no cognitive ability left.

Next, the infected individual's motor functions are severely damaged causing tremors, loss of balance, equilibrium, and neurodegeneration. Ultimately the disorder will result in the host's death, causing the person infected to become almost as a zombie in appearance and actions.

The undead rises from the cold earth to terrorize those who placed them there. Is this a

---

[55] https://medlineplus.gov/ency/article/001379.htm

SANCTUM OF SHADOWS · SPIRITUS OCCULTUS

BEDTIME STORY TO KEEP CHILDREN AWAKE ALL NIGHT OR IS IT TRULY ROOTED IN FACTUAL OCCURRENCES FROM OUR ANIMALISTIC HISTORY?

WHAT DO YOU THINK?

Ave Versus Christi

"We cannot see the wind and yet it carries things in a molecular fashion, demonstrating great power. We have not fully harnessed the wind but, claiming the wind does not exist simply because you do not see it, is to turn a blind eye to a principle that is known; of which the effects can be clearly seen."[56]

Aleister Nacht

One of the most important attributes for the practitioner of magic is <u>focus</u>. The person who can focus precisely on that which needs to be addressed while locking out everything else around them will certainly be successful in magical endeavors.

Being aware of one's surroundings is important however, there are times during every magical operation when energy must be directly focused in order to receive the return on investment for the time and energy. We are discussing abstractions and a person must have the capability to turn the abstract into reality.

Many magical practitioners develop this

---

[56] *Sanctum of Shadows Volume II*

ability through trial and error; having practiced numerous times until finding the proverbial "sweet spot". This is a subtle division of attention and at the right moment, a laser-focus on the task at hand. These practitioners become very competent in their practice because they know when to "turn up the heat".

Many magical operations are similar to mathematic or chemistry equations. Knowing how to put the equation together is just as important as the correct answer or solution. If you do not have the knowledge needed in order to perform certain magical operations, those magical elements will escape your grasp and you will not be successful because you do not completely understand.

As with any art or science, magic has limitations and knowing those limitations will certainly keep the practitioner out of trouble. Magic deals with forces of energy and just like a lightning bolt which comes from the clouds, magic has the same intensity and capacity for creating damage.

The practitioner must know how to capture, channel, and focus energy with controlling activities in order to raise the energy level, focus that energy, and perform the magical operations. Controlling the energy needed for

THE ACTIONS AND EXPECTED OUTCOME REQUIRES MASTERY. THE PRACTITIONER WILL NEVER MOVE BEYOND THE ROTE LEARNING NEOPHYTE WITHOUT THIS MASTERY.

SATHANAS

Epilogus

I always seem to have some personal notes which do not fit well in my books. For this reason, I find the Epilogus to be the perfect location to summarize and / or expand upon certain thoughts. This book is no different.

While writing this manuscript I found my usual methodology inadequate. In the past, I began with a thought, expanded the thought into elements, addressed each element, and moved to the next chapter. This book was different and while it consumed more time to write, I feel the process facilitated a "deeper dive" into each thought.

My perspective is sometimes difficult to articulate and sometimes even more difficult to consume. For me, the analogy of "the words get in the way" certainly applies to some ideas and concepts. How can awareness be properly communicated to an infant? How can magick be thoroughly explained to a roudy congress of baboons? How can a delicious gormet meal be properly delivered at the drive-through window?

Frustration is ever-present while I write a new book. At times, I wrestle with line after line which is creatively paralyzing. There is immeasurable amounts of information just beyond the locked door. Unfortunately, words are the key which opens the door. Finding the right sequence and phrase becomes the challenge to be accepted and overcome. As I have said before "Words are tools that build ideas". The unfathomable cries out to be understood!

Another challenge was to put my manager's betrayal behind me and heal the wound. When someone steals from you, it becomes very difficult to trust anyone else. The event and subsequent "fallout" zapped my strength and doused my creative flame. I felt numb inside and among the pieces of wreckage was bitterness. I was justified in the end, collected the money taken, and the legal issues settled yet, I felt totally empty.

Gathering my thoughts into something productive has been a real challenge indeed. I gaze at the Gulf of Mexico and my mind wanders into fantasy.

My constant craving to write has been subdued by my "hate" and I have suppressed the call of the words for too long. While this may not be my best book, it has certainly been successful; forcing me to write again. To those who have checked on me from time to time: "Thank you! This is book is for you."

SCIRE QUOD SCIENDUM

AD HOMINEM - Argument directed against a person rather than the position they are maintaining.

ANALYSIS PARALYSIS - The state of over-analyzing (or over-thinking) a situation so that a decision or action is never taken, in effect paralyzing the outcome.

ATHAME - A double-edged ritual knife used in modern Witchcraft and Satanism.

AURIC - Of or relating to the aura supposedly surrounding a living creature.

AUTO-DA-FÉ - The ritual of public penance of condemned heretics and apostates.

BAPHOMET - Baphomet (/ˈbæfɵmɛt/; from Medieval Latin Baphometh, Baffometi, Occitan Bafometz) is an imagined pagan deity (i.e., a product of Xtian folklore concerning pagans), revived in the 19th century as a figure of occultism and Satanism. It first appeared in 11th and 12th century Latin and Provençal as a corruption of "Mahomet", the Latinisation of "Muhammad", but later it appeared as a term for a pagan idol in trial transcripts of the Inquisition of the Knights Templar in the early 14th century. The name first came into popular English-speaking consciousness in the 19th century, with debate and speculation on the reasons for the suppression of the Templars.

Black Magic - Magic involving the supposed invocation of evil spirits or demons for evil purposes.

Black Mass - Ritual of the Church of Satan; performed to blaspheme and free the participants from the hold of anything widely accepted as sacred, not just organized religion, as in the traditional Black Mass which is meant as a blasphemy against Catholicism. (aka Messe Noire)

SANCTUM OF SHADOWS · SPIRITUS OCCULTUS

Caveat Emptor - The principle that the buyer alone is responsible for checking the quality and suitability of goods before a purchase is made.

Chakra - Chakra are believed to be centers of the body from which a person can collect energy. They are connected to major organs or glands that govern other body parts.

Chalice - A chalice (from Latin calix, cup, borrowed from Greek kalyx, shell, husk) is a goblet or footed cup intended to hold a drink. In general religious terms, it is intended for drinking during a ceremony.

Coitus Interruptus - Also known as the rejected sexual intercourse, withdrawal or pullout method, is a method of birth-control in which a man, during intercourse withdraws his penis from a woman's vagina prior to ejaculation. The man then directs his ejaculate (semen) away from his partner's vagina to avoid

INSEMINATION.

CONCUBINE - CONCUBINAGE IS AN INTERPERSONAL RELATIONSHIP IN WHICH A PERSON ENGAGES IN AN ONGOING RELATIONSHIP (USUALLY MATRIMONIALLY ORIENTED) WITH ANOTHER PERSON TO WHOM THEY ARE NOT OR CANNOT BE MARRIED; THE INABILITY TO MARRY IS USUALLY DUE TO A DIFFERENCE IN SOCIAL STATUS OR ECONOMIC CONDITION. HISTORICALLY, THE RELATIONSHIP INVOLVED A MAN IN A HIGHER STATUS POSITION, USUALLY WITH A LEGALLY SANCTIONED SPOUSE, WHO MAINTAINS A SECOND HOUSEHOLD WITH THE LESSER "SPOUSE". THE WOMAN IN SUCH A RELATIONSHIP IS REFERRED TO AS A CONCUBINE.

CONJURE - TO MAKE (SOMETHING) APPEAR UNEXPECTEDLY OR SEEMINGLY FROM NOWHERE AS BY MAGIC.

COVEN - A GROUP OR GATHERING OF WITCHES OR SATANISTS WHO MEET REGULARLY.

CRONE - HIGH RANKING MEMBER OF A SATANIC COVEN. ASSISTS AND ADVISES THE COVEN HIGH PRIESTESS

SANCTUM OF SHADOWS · SPIRITUS OCCULTUS

ON MAGIC, RITUAL AND COVEN HISTORICAL ACCOUNTS.

DEDUCTIVE REASONING - LOGICAL PROCESS IN WHICH A CONCLUSION IS BASED ON THE CONCORDANCE OF MULTIPLE PREMISES THAT ARE GENERALLY ASSUMED TO BE TRUE. (TOP-DOWN LOGIC).

DEMONOLOGY - THE STUDY OF DEMONS OR OF DEMONIC BELIEF.

DIVINE COMEDY - THE DIVINE COMEDY (ITALIAN: DIVINA COMMEDIA) IS AN EPIC POEM WRITTEN BY DANTE ALIGHIERI BETWEEN 1308 AND HIS DEATH IN 1321.

DUBIOUS AUTHORITY - FALLACY OF CITING A PERSON WHO IS NOT REALLY AN AUTHORITY ON THE SUBJECT MATTER AT ISSUE.

ENLIGHTENMENT - THE ACTION OF ENLIGHTENING OR THE STATE OF BEING ENLIGHTENED THROUGH UNDERSTANDING, AWARENESS, WISDOM, EDUCATION, LEARNING, OR KNOWLEDGE.

EVOCATION - THE ACT OF CALLING OR SUMMONING A SPIRIT, DEMON, GOD OR OTHER supernatural agent, in the Western Mystery tradition. Comparable practices exist in many religions and magical traditions and may use potions with and without uttered word formulas.

Fasching - The German carnival season.

Grimoire - A Grimoire is a description of a set of magical symbols / actions and how to combine them properly.

Habit (cloth) - A long, loose garment worn by a member of a religious order or congregation.

Hell - A place regarded in various religions as a spiritual realm of evil and suffering, often traditionally depicted as a place of perpetual fire beneath the earth where the wicked are punished after death.

Higher Magic - Higher order of cognitive and magical abilities.

Incantation - A series of words said as a

MAGIC SPELL.

INCUBUS - A male demon that has sexual intercourse with sleeping women.

INDUCTIVE REASONING - Logical process in which multiple premises, all believed true or found true most of the time, are combined to obtain a specific conclusion.

INNER SANCTUM - The most sacred place of magical workings for a coven.

INVALID ARGUMENT - Argument in which the premises provide unsound reasons for the conclusion.

INVERTED PENTAGRAM - A five-pointed star that is formed by drawing a continuous line in five straight segments, often used as a mystic and magical symbol. Often used by occult practitioners.

INVOCATION - The action of invoking something or someone for assistance or as an authority. An invocation (from the Latin verb

INVOCARE "TO CALL ON, INVOKE, TO GIVE") MAY TAKE THE FORM OF: SUPPLICATION, PRAYER OR SPELL. A FORM OF POSSESSION.

COMMAND OR CONJURATION.

SELF-IDENTIFICATION WITH CERTAIN SPIRITS.

LEX TALIONIS - LAW OF THE JUNGLE OR THE TALON. THE NATURAL ORDER WHERE THE WEAK ARE ALLOWED TO PERISH, THE STRONG SURVIVE. DARWIN'S SURVIVAL OF THE FITTEST.

LHP - LEFT-HAND PATH, IS A TERM USED IN THE WESTERN ESOTERICISM.

LOUP-GAROU - A PERSON CURSED TO LIVE AS A LYCANTHROPE. (AKA WEREWOLF).

MESSE NOIRE - SEE BLACK MASS.

MISOLOGY - THE HATRED OF REASONING; THE REVULSION OR DISTRUST OF LOGICAL DEBATE, ARGUMENTATION, OR THE SOCRATIC METHOD.

MODUS PONENS - RULE OF LOGIC STATING THAT IF A CONDITIONAL STATEMENT (IF P THEN Q) IS ACCEPTED, AND THE ANTECEDENT (P) HOLDS, THEN THE

CONSEQUENT (Q) MAY BE INFERRED.

MODUS TOLLENS - RULE OF LOGIC STATING THAT IF A CONDITIONAL STATEMENT (IF P THEN Q) IS ACCEPTED, AND THE CONSEQUENT DOES NOT HOLD (NOT-Q), THEN THE NEGATION OF THE ANTECEDENT (NOT-P) CAN BE INFERRED.

NEOPHYTE - A PERSON WHO IS NEW TO A SUBJECT, SKILL, OR BELIEF.

NOLA - NEW ORLEANS, LOUISIANA.

NOSTRADAMUS - MICHEL DE NOSTREDAME, USUALLY LATINISED AS NOSTRADAMUS, WAS A FRENCH APOTHECARY AND REPUTED SEER WHO PUBLISHED COLLECTIONS OF PROPHECIES THAT HAVE SINCE BECOME FAMOUS WORLDWIDE. HE IS BEST KNOWN FOR HIS BOOK "LES PROPHETIES" (THE PROPHECIES), THE FIRST EDITION OF WHICH APPEARED IN 1555. SINCE THE PUBLICATION OF THIS BOOK, WHICH HAS RARELY BEEN OUT OF PRINT SINCE HIS DEATH, NOSTRADAMUS HAS ATTRACTED A FOLLOWING THAT, ALONG WITH MUCH OF THE POPULAR PRESS, CREDITS HIM WITH PREDICTING MANY MAJOR WORLD EVENTS.

ORGASM - A CLIMAX OF SEXUAL EXCITEMENT, CHARACTERIZED BY FEELINGS OF PLEASURE CENTERED IN THE GENITALS AND (IN MEN) EXPERIENCED AS AN ACCOMPANIMENT TO EJACULATION.

POSER - ANARCHISTS WHO HIDE BEHIND SATANISM TO SATISFY THEIR OWN DESTRUCTIVE DESIRES; NOT THOSE OF SATAN.

RITE - A RELIGIOUS OR OTHER SOLEMN CEREMONY OR ACT.

RITUALE ROMANUM - THE ROMAN RITUAL (LATIN: RITUALE ROMANUM) IS ONE OF THE OFFICIAL RITUAL WORKS OF THE ROMAN RITE OF THE CATHOLIC CHURCH. IT CONTAINS ALL THE SERVICES WHICH MAY BE PERFORMED BY A PRIEST OR DEACON WHICH ARE NOT CONTAINED WITHIN EITHER THE MISSALE ROMANUM OR THE BREVARIUM ROMANUM. THE BOOK ALSO CONTAINS SOME OF THE RITES WHICH ARE CONTAINED IN ONLY ONE OF THESE BOOKS FOR CONVENIENCE.

SAMAEL - SAMAEL (HEBREW: סמאל) (ALSO SAMMAEL AND SAMIL) IS AN IMPORTANT ARCHANGEL

IN TALMUDIC AND POST-TALMUDIC LORE, A FIGURE WHO IS ACCUSER, SEDUCER AND DESTROYER, AND HAS BEEN REGARDED AS BOTH GOOD AND EVIL.

SEX MAGIC - SEX MAGIC IS A TERM FOR VARIOUS TYPES OF SEXUAL ACTIVITY USED IN MAGICAL, RITUALISTIC, OR OTHERWISE RELIGIOUS AND SPIRITUAL PURSUITS. ONE PRACTICE OF SEX MAGIC IS USING THE ENERGY OF SEXUAL AROUSAL OR ORGASM WITH VISUALIZATION OF A DESIRED RESULT. A PREMISE OF SEX MAGIC IS THE IDEA THAT SEXUAL ENERGY IS A POTENT FORCE THAT CAN BE HARNESSED TO TRANSCEND ONE'S NORMALLY PERCEIVED REALITY. ORAL, VAGINAL, ANAL AND OTHER METHODS ARE EMPLOYED DURING SEX MAGIC RITUALS.

SHEMHAMFORASH - THE SHEMHAMPHORASCH IS A CORRUPTION OF THE HEBREW TERM SHEM HA-MEPHORASH (שם המפורש), WHICH WAS USED IN TANNAITIC TIMES TO REFER TO THE TETRAGRAMMATON. IN EARLY KABBALAH THE TERM WAS USED TO DESIGNATE SOMETIMES A SEVENTY-TWO LETTER NAME FOR GOD, and sometimes a forty-two letter name. Rashi said Shem ha-Mephorash was used for a forty-two letter name, but Maimonides thought Shem ha-Mephorash was used only for the four letter Tetragrammaton.

Socratic Method - The Socratic method (also known as method of elenchus, elenctic method, Socratic irony, or Socratic debate), named after the classical Greek philosopher Socrates, is a form of inquiry and debate between individuals with opposing viewpoints based on asking and answering questions to stimulate critical thinking and to illuminate ideas. It is a dialectical method, often involving an oppositional discussion in which the defense of one point of view is pitted against the defense of another; one participant may lead another to contradict himself in some way, thus strengthening the inquirer's own point.

Succubus - A female demon believed to have sexual intercourse with sleeping men.

SWOT Analysis - A useful technique for understanding your Strengths and Weaknesses, and for identifying both the Opportunities open to you and the Threats you face.

Syllogism - a form of reasoning in which a conclusion is drawn (whether validly or not) from two given or assumed propositions (premises), each of which shares a term with the conclusion, and shares a common or middle term not present in the conclusion.

Tautology - saying of the same thing twice in different words, generally considered to be a fault of style.

Third Eye - The innate ability to sense and understand more than meets the eye.

Thurible - A thurible is a metal censer suspended from chains, in which incense is burned during worship services.

Thurifer - The person who carries the thurible.

Vampire - Those beings (undead or living

CREATURE) WHO SURVIVE BY FEEDING ON THE BLOOD OF LIVING CREATURES.

VALID ARGUMENT - THE TRUTH OF THE PREMISES LOGICALLY GUARANTEES THE TRUTH OF THE CONCLUSION.

WIMPLE - A CLOTH HEADDRESS COVERING THE HEAD, THE NECK, AND THE SIDES OF THE FACE, FORMERLY WORN BY WOMEN AND STILL WORN BY SOME NUNS.

SANCTUM OF SHADOWS · SPIRITUS OCCULTUS

Ecce Homo

Author Aleister Nacht is a Satanic Magus and leader of Magnum Opus, a Satanic coven comprising of numerous groups.

With a modern view of Satanism, he brings the darkness to life in a very tangible manner. His books have found favor with a multitude of searchers crossing all demographic and worldwide geographic boundaries. Aleister Nacht lives in the Tampa Bay area and enjoys the "Salt Life".

You can find more information about Aleister Nacht on his website.
www.AleisterNacht.com

Aleister Nacht's Satanic Magic Blog contains a wealth of information about Satanism and Devil Worship.
www.SatanicMagic.Wordpress.com

Made in the USA
Columbia, SC
09 March 2025